THE HIDDEN DIARIES
OF A NUBIAN GODDESS

THE HIDDEN DIARIES OF A NUBIAN GODDESS

ZEELAYAH MONK

PALMETTO
P U B L I S H I N G
Charleston, SC
www.PalmettoPublishing.com

Copyright © 2023 by Zeelayah Monk

All rights reserved
No portion of this book may be reproduced, stored in a retrieval system, or transmitted in any form by any means–electronic, mechanical, photocopy, recording, or other–except for brief quotations in printed reviews, without prior permission of the author.

Paperback ISBN: 979-8-8229-3308-8

Table of Contents

Divine Consciousness..1
Thousands Of Poets 2
My Inner City's Blues 3
City Breeds.. 4
From Yours Truly.. 6
I'll Get Out...8
Blood Family..10
A Slaves Song 11
A Woman on a Mission 12
The Grand Change of It All 14
War On Femininity 15
Hallway 11 16
The Prayer Set In Stone 18
Becoming Woman...19
What kind of woman will I be 20
The Intro 21
The Break Down 22
The Body 23
The Outro... 24
What Is A Man..25
Beautiful Man..27
Dear Future Husband 28
A Good Man 29
Nothing Sweeter.. 30
What Is Love?...32

- Intimacy ... 33
- When We Make Love ... 34
- As We Lay ... 35
- A little Girls Cry ... 36
- Damaged Petals ... 37
- Your Love ... 38
- Our Love ... 40
- Broken Hearted Soul ... 41
- Pure Soul ... 42
- If Home Is Where the Heart Is ... 44
- A scar on My Heart ... 45
- An Impaired Mind ... 46
- Steady Flow Of Self-Love ... 47
- Men Suffer in Silence ... 48
- Flow Of Life ... 49
- Why Does the River Need The Rain? ... 50
- Divine Flow ... 51
- Sitting In The Rain ... 52
- The Sun & The Moon ... 53
- I Wonder ... 54
- Cold Feet ... 55
- I'm Stuck ... 56
- I am who I say I am ... 57
- Count Your Blessings ... 58
- Forgiveness ... 59
- My own Fears ... 60
- Iniquity ... 61

I Care For You 62
I'm in Love 63
My Motivation 64
Save Me 65
Subconscious Dump 66

Divine Consciousness

God is in everything we do and say all that we think and speak
I like to think of God as the imagination
There's no limits to creation here
I imagine God in my mind visualizing me as its form of creation
A divine form of expression
Everything that I think and do is divinely orchestrated
I am operating from a space of divine consciousness
A blank space everything that could be exists here
This is my original state of being
This is who I was before I was conditioned into what is acceptable for me to show up as in my being

Thousands Of Poets

There are thousands of poets
Intentionally
I want my name to be one for the books
A poet who speaks to, touches your soul
A poet who's pen against paper gives you healing
Feeling high spirits
A poet who speaks for the voiceless
A poet whose vision speaks for the children
I believe we're all here moving to make a difference
I just want to be that poet whose words were felt

My Inner City's Blues

A sense of community is what's missing
Like the days when the next-door neighbor can watch your kids while you're gone
Teach them about who they are and how to respect themselves, in the way they show up
I miss the days when the block was hot not from gun shots
Baby girls lined up playing hopscotch
Young kings having conversations about what new kicks just dropped
Great mother I ask you bring back the days when our community gave us our backbones
I'm so tired of seeing our babies drop like flies
From these ashes I have high hopes
We will rise
Hear the cry of mama screaming and hollering about the blood that was shed in her baby's demise
Same tears she shed, be the blood in which she bled on her time of the month
The daye I heard Gaye's blues of the inner city my heart started to holler and say bring back what we once called a peaceful day

City Breeds

The city breeds soldiers' boys turn men from cold nights girls turn women becomes vice
I would believe it's a journey within itself, boxed in feels as if the walls slowly keep closing in
No matter what this life looks like
No matter what was given to you know that you were made to display your own sense of self
Your strength is never hidden it's in all that you do it's seen baby girl your worth so much more than how many wandering eyes you can spot and find
Young man you illuminate don't get caught up with the wrong one
Time will past by and you'll end up living a life that feels like you're on a downward slope
You are your mother's son but even to her you don't owe your life you're a gem
Precious
They don't make em like you no more like you went out of style
You were chosen to bring back what's missing your presence is essential to the kingdom meaningful when it comes to my heart
Influential to the little baby girl's and baby boys' life's in which you touched , you are significant to natures flow
Baby girl you are connected as one with the heart beat the flow of the great mother
The one we call mother nature your cycles are tied into the mother up above the one that lights up the night time sky

Even when you feel unbalanced, I want you to know you always are

You are divine flow being expressed in a matter of cellular vibration

A magnificent creation I hope you feel what I'm saying

From Yours Truly

Mama, what is it that you're trying to tell me?
Is it that little girl born to the North Philly streets who raised me
Baby girl that was stripped of her childhood took on the role of her siblings' caregiver
That little girl that was pushed out on her own told her strength would get her through
Please, tell me mama was this little girl the one who was mothering me all along because I swear I see her in me when I can't seem to figure out what's wrong
Fourteen, found out you were carrying a seed but had a much bigger dream
Young black Queen on the track team
baby girl was a star in the making
I see in you what you wanted everyone else to see
If you would've took the risk to be self-full, choose yourself
I know you would be living the beautiful life you always dreamed
Birthed by a woman who struggled with addiction crack fiend
I hear the little girl in you cry and say I think I'm still just trying to wake up
I can blame it all on being a dream maybe if I wish hard enough, I could get a chance to go back
This time the power would lie only in my hands it would start with me actually getting to just be a little kid

I was forged into womanhood not knowing a thing I hear you say "mom I'm calling out to you, don't you hear my sorrows" here today could be gone by tomorrow

At nineteen lost your love to the prison system sat through every hearing in your heart you felt to be the victim

The victim of the justice system who came in and broke up the last thing you haven't lost hope in from that day on you struggled with what life has been

Longing for your man and the kids that could've been opening your legs to a man is not a sin

Forget about all the ones who sat around, played make pretend Counting your downfalls

Silent upon all your wins by beating you down talking about you like a dog they created their own sin

Mama I know your still just a little girl, turned woman overnight but I still would like to see her win

Know that this was written from the heart of your daughter through this life I hope we're able to stay friends

I'll Get Out

I want to get out
Go to a place that doesn't make me feel like a slave without physical chains
No master

Go to a place where bondage doesn't flow through my veins
keeping me tied to what keeps me going insane

Got me feeling like the blood that pours out of each of my veins
are a representation of every last ancestor
whose voice was taken in an imperceptible way

They whisper to me when I sleep at night
Sing to me chants of empowerment
this here wakes me up as if I was rising from the dead
This is how I'm able to make it through

I'll get out

The biggest mistake was putting me in a box I made by hand
I could be a prisoner in my own cell
made of ones who became my best friends

Doubt
Fear

Running in my veins at a rapid pace
damn near next to kin

Do you hear what I'm telling you

Young pharaoh went to war within himself
didn't need nothing more than his own brain
Killed himself in a one-on-one war

I won't let none of your names die in vain
Ill carry the dreams of the ones who came before me
So at night I pray for all these lonely nights to be a sense of comfort

In no way that keeps me the same

Blood Family

Blood don't make you family
You can be raised under the same roof yet govern under different moral codes
Raised around ones who's hearts were made of stone
Even though we not the same
I feel, I carry the pain of my brothers and sisters' wrongs
You just ran across my mind so it got me thinking
Sitting here wondering how the day would look when you have to face all the lies you've been keeping
Been my sisters keeper for so long its hard for my eyes to keep from bleeding

A Slaves Song

Why does a slave sing?

Held hostage in the battlefield of one's mind
Even here is not enough to keep the spirit of this soul down

A slave sings not from a place of chains no, not at all
A slave's voice is its freedom it's connection to the most high

The power that's spoken out into the universe from that slave's mouth
is enough to let the caged birds fly free
With damaged and freshly clipped wings

Why does a slave sing?

No matter how far they kick us down we find a way to multiply
Our song is why the world keeps turning round and round
A slave's song is the backbone to everything we call our own

A Woman on a Mission

Your art can only be as alive as you are
So that makes me ask what am I?
Where does my creativity lie

At times I'm catching a vibe and other times I can't even hitch a ride
I get to a point where I'm consumed by the outside distractions and it then becomes fatal to my words of inspiration

Can my words be felt in a way where its healing to oneself?
I want to just make it with the cards I was dealt
only to realize I was the one that dealt them to myself,
expecting change from someone other than the one I see ,
observing self

Anyway, as a being I'm just supposed to love on myself and not expect anyone to do the same
I can trust in me

If I change it'll be beneficial to the one staring back at me
Looking into the mirror its reflecting self

I'm in between
Out here just tryna make a way
Not working for me

Following the norm is not for me
At 9 I'm ready mind made up focused on the execution
By 5 I'm listening to myself asking what the hell am I really doing?

I'm lacking on the job, I've aborted the mission
I'm a woman with a vision it's all conducive if I continue
to go out my way to do something I have no business doing

My heart and mind will begin to be poisoned

The Grand Change of It All

How can I be grounded in the same place I'm being uprooted?
The great change
Knocking at my window blowing in the sweet smell of freedom
Cradling me as if I am a newborn baby
Feeding me the milk of infinite wisdom nurturing my soul nursing me back to life my roots became dry and brittle from combat
The sight of black butterflies multiplying before my eyes reminding me that no matter how dark it gets, I still have the ability to fly

War On Femininity

There's a war on femininity
She's been
Her truth had been buried underneath so many lies
Her presence, deemed and under handedly broken down its unseen
How can the feminine rise if we don't know the way
tell me how can we grow from that little princess into a woman without the proper training
Our womanhood is supposed to be lived out in our day-to-day
But I ask again
How do we restore the flow if we weren't taught the natural way we were conditioned to be any and everything expect for our natural being
Good looks, banging bodies, and pieces of steel we became its slave
Our feminine energy has been under attack since we were bought in trade
I pray my sisters be freed
Our way is not their way that's why we feel like we're going insane
Been out of touch with ourselves so long we believe just about anything they have to say
Believe me when I know
you'll know the same

Hallway 11

I'm sitting in hallway eleven with nothing more than a deep thought
Why am I here?
What has brought me to this?
I sit as I watch others pass by
Person, after person
One conversation after another I start to think am I being felt?
Seems as if I'm not even here
Here for one problem yet I seem to have uncovered another
What I needed wasn't what I came here for
For what I needed is all that I came here for Hallway eleven sat there for hours, energy drained my life force was being taken from
I realized that sometimes sickness that comes about isn't from what we think and know
Sometimes it can be energetically, spiritually
It can't be found in the body
I'm sitting in hallway eleven realizing I am spiritually sick from the energy's that I've allowed to take from my life source from the ones I let in my inner world
This has now manifested into pain, into disease
Sitting here in hallway eleven I realize I have many things but one reigns supreme, my dream
A dream of me living a life that is beneficial to my soul's path
No one but no one can deliver what I can while on this path

Sitting in hallway eleven realizing all I have is me at the end of the day the outside sources are just a support of me an extension of me
Yea, I can see my reflection in them but it still always goes back to just me
I'm sitting in hallway eleven realizing I just got to let things be
I can't feel a sense of entitlement just because I feel I should have it, or cause it feels good
Sometimes the very person, place, or thing was placed in your life just to give you a glimpse of what's to come
Doesn't mean you have to hold on to the thing that was posed as an example before you get what you've been waiting for, your prize possession
Hallway eleven showed me all I am is purpose, divine flow
What I have can't be broken only multiplied one in a million something they'll kill for
A healer
I can heal myself
It's bigger than me
Greater than my feelings and what I think I know
I look in my eyes and see a certain glow
That glow is universal speaks through me something from outer space god given yeah, you know
The moment you act like you don't it starts to show

The Prayer Set In Stone

I aspire to be what I was born to be and that's a natural woman
The feeling of being unequipped has brought me to a feeling of despair
I feel the little girl in me fighting, to prove that she can be a woman
A natural woman
That little girl feels like she has something to prove
I've given power to the ones who impelled on my journey entering into womanhood
Now I find myself on a internal battle with my present self and
The baby girl that cries out from a broken heart
Do I have what it takes to be a natural woman?
A woman who knows how to operate and show up as a woman
That's all I want to be
A natural woman
Could the ancestors grant the wish of thee

Becoming Woman

Coming into womanhood isn't common to be easily defined
Especially when you find yourself doubting what lives within
constantly having people in my ear telling me I'm not there yet
Got me in an ongoing cycle of trying to arrive growing, but not fast enough
Learning, but it's not seasoned enough
I feel like my womanhood isn't enough
Comments on my "young age" got me moving in ego with something to prove
I'm past the princess stage I'm no longer a little girl
Here and now I'm in the space of discovering self and becoming my own woman
To you I have nothing at all to prove my womanhood isn't up for discussion of your voiced opinions

What kind of woman will I be

What kind of woman will I be? When I'm unsure of what a woman truly is
What kind of woman will I be if I lack self-respect?
I can't help but think I'm supposed to spread myself thin
I say yes when I really mean no, give myself to you when she's telling me no
What type of woman will I be if I've only seen a woman do it all on her own
Never seen a complete union that's safe, quiet and I get to call my own
Might I ask again? What kind of woman will I be? What kind of woman am I? What kind of woman do I want to be?
What kind of woman will I be if I ever was to fall in love
I'm afraid to say but I'm unsure of how a woman is supposed to truly love
How is she supposed to treat her man?
How do I talk to him in a way in which he understands? I don't wish to be little him, make him feel less of a man
I desire to be his peace even when we might be speaking a language we both don't seem to understand

The Intro

I know
I know you've heard the talk about women
I know you were taught and conditioned to judge her based on how she walks, talks, by her looks or even by what she clothes herself in
I know, I know
You think she's meant to be controlled she'd be far to lost on her own
The limitations of your mind is what got you viewing her from a point of glaucoma
She's far more than what your daddy or momma might have told ya
She's not all about the commas or drama but more about healing what's been blocked up inside her, and I comma
Do you know she is life's secret hidden in plain sight?
Do you know her as the start and end of any and every light? Your life?
Do you know she's the reason why you even have a will or even the right to fight?
If you knew what I knew I'd believe you'll reevaluate your whole life
You'll know (she) is
L-I-F-E

The Break Down

What is a woman?
What is womb man?
My response to that would be simple, one word
L-I-F-E
So then what is life?
Breath
Which is connected to the heart
What is heart? Its home
We can never get put out of it but also it's the only place we are not afraid of shutting ourselves out of
Heart, is also mother
A internal representation of our mother she plays the role of our life giver our door to the most precious thing Life
Which brings me back to where I started what is a woman
Womb man
I can tell you what she is what she means to me

The Body

One might say she's soft in nature
Loving to self and all that lives
I'd say she's careful of who she gives herself to
Nurturing to all living things patience with life (self) as well as kids
Guided by divine innergy
Honest even when it's hard to be
Respectful of others and her temple
Strong when moving through emotions
Successful in what she deems be
Thoughtful in all situations
Resourceful in nature
Healing, for others surrounding her and who she comes in contact with and most importantly always for (her) self
One might say (she) is home, brings feelings of security in all
Mother would say (she) respects and honors her love, the divine masculine

The Outro

I would ask you, open your mind and heart to ask your (self)
who is womb man?
Who is SHE?
She plays a specific role in all of our lives
A role not all plays out the same
Some of us might feel like some way somehow, we need an exchange
Reality is, sometimes the main character just can't embody the role often times it's because they've never been told
Do you know there's value in every role
Let's just extend some grace and just simply say
Momma just never known

What Is A Man

What is a man? He is life force
Yes (life) representing meaning the woman
Force being the stability behind it
The backbone, strength
A man is POWER
In the most demonstrative way he can also be seen as the foundation in all that you see

The break down starts with what a man means to me

A man is
Honest in all situations
A man is caring in nature
A man is loving it comes from his heart
It's pure and calming
He's also nurturing, it's in his nature
Dependable when need be, as well as in every situation
Determine to achieve his goals
Believe-able when times are hard
Selfless when need be
Charming when I'm down
Successful in all he does
Liberating in the most darkest times, and always for (him) self
He's gentle, it's in his nature
With woman, children, he's gentle in spirit

My man, he's a peacemaker, A peace bringer , all I can tell you is when things seem uptight not right or uncomfortable

He brings warmth to and where ever he goes

He respects, honors and loves the divine feminine energy and the land in which she rules over

(He) is one of a kind

(He) can't be denied see a man can't just be created he has to be defined

A man becomes, and when he does

It's a force to be reckoned with

A man IS!

Beautiful Man

Have you ever seen a beautiful man before?
It was your eyes that captured me
A sight of a man with such a big heart
A lover, A provider

When I see you I see a heavy weight that you may have been carrying quite long I must say

You've been beaten down ...
I know
You don't know for sure ...
I know
You've been hurt before ...
I know

Your eyes, they speak to me
Your eyes, they comfort me
Your eyes, like a river something within just runs so deep

The scars on your outer layer simply reflect scars from within
Your so much more than what meets the eye, so powerful, just a beautiful man
I know you'll grow into who you truly are
Until then, I'll love you from a far
Entitled a beautiful man

Dear Future Husband

How has your journey been
I want to know the depths of your heart
The depths of your soul
I want to know all that you've been through and how it has shaped you
into the man I see standing before me present day
My dear, how do you see the world?
What does life mean to you?
What do you hold dear to you
I'm talking morally
How did you learn to get back up once you were kicked down
How did you establish your connection with the divine?
Do you know how and when to nurture me
pour into a woman like me
My being needs to be treated like a garden
different compartments in need of different treatment
this is how my being has to be attended to
I'll give nourishment to all of your being too
this is not a one-way street no give and pull

A Good Man

A good man
I don't want a rough neck
I don't want a man that's in a mental prison
Beating his chest flexing money
It has impressed the rest
Neither do I need my man barking on some DMX
I don't wish to chase BMX
I want to come home to my man in the kitchen cooking up love
My mind is laid at ease
An nonpareil love
Love making peerless
Inimitable feel of home with you

Nothing Sweeter

Someone came along one day and asked me what was the sweetest thing I ever known
I don't plan to kick it to you like Ms. Lauryn but I will paint a clear picture
So that you know
They always say when you meet "the one"
You'll know
I thought of it to be cliché like it was something that everyone liked to say
Your presence illuminated my whole inner world
Like a little girl you had me blushing and just like that the energy of love came rushing in as if it was an emergency
If my life was on the line you came in and gave me vital nutrients
Restorative
Reviving
Therapeutic
To my whole being a simple touch around my waist
Breathtaking
I can't let this go to waste I know we both got things we have to grow from
This way we will be more peaceful to live with
In need of the proper space, it will all be worth it when I see the day my vision is lived out
Maybe a child by this time would have come about

A little boy with the heart of his mother and the spirit of his father a young man on a mission
He is in no need of permission
God gave him all he would need no wishing
The sweetest thing I ever known we planted a seed and overtime watched it grow
The intent was there so this time around it shows
I always knew giving it time was the best way to go
I love you baby; I wish to never kiss you goodbye
If I were, A piece of me would be left unsatisfied
Think about you all the time I love your eyes
Every time I see you they singing to me or spitting a different rhyme ... every time
So fine
Worth more than a dime, for your worth to be expressed a dime would have to be multiplied about a thousand times
Young black King
On a rise

What Is Love?

What is love? This question is a deep one
When I ask myself, it always brings upon me some silence
No matter how many times I ask myself I can't seem to stick with just one answer
Love, L-O-V-E
Something about it just makes my heart shake to me
it seems as if it's a supernatural element that humans just so happen to be blessed with
Not to be used as a weapon
What is love?
An undying feeling, could bring you high sometimes low
But when it's there you'll know
I feel it in my heart, the feel of butterflies in your chest
True and honest
Gentle and caring
Soft spoken
Never harsh or boastful
Don't mistaken love for what's actually just a learning lesson
you must not mistake it for something you chose from a place of brokenness
Love is uplifting love is sweet
To the ears it sounds as a soft harmony pair with a simple melody
To the eyes it looks like an unexpected rainbow

Intimacy

He explores the most deepest, and inner parts of me
I hold on tight as he enters the most sensual part of my being
Every moment of our love making is filled with love
He is the truth in which I choose to stand in
With, By
He is the one I've been longing for
Not virgin but I've never been able to open up to a man in this way before
you're the reason I don't equate pain with love anymore
you have shown me the beauty of a man
what a man truly exists for
Mon amour , you are indeed everything I was in search for

When We Make Love

When we make love, I see into you
I become you
When we make love, I feel free
You feel me, you see me , you come to realize , you are me
Long before this moment we were intertwined to me it's beyond me being yours
Even if you were with another the fact is, you can't replace something that's already been divinely orchestrated
I am your wife before the ring, you are my husband before the bended knee
When we make love, I flow rivers of pain that was stored long before we reunited
This pain, dissipates within every stroke that you give sexual healing, this pain you take from me
You tell me, now that you're here there's no more fears
You took this pain away and turned it to evolution
You supported me in my transformation
It has now just begun

As We Lay

Can I lay with you before we make love
Can I caress you with my gentle touch, can I feel you I promise I don't want to rush
Your worth so much beyond just a quick rush
There's so much power within you, you make me want to explode
The touch of your back, the feel of your chest I know what this leads to next
Hold on, before we do , can I ask you a simple question in hopes that this sets the mood
"When's the last time you made love"
I ask of you
I would make love to you only if you asked me to
I want to nurture and heal you
This is what my love gives and is
I want to look into your eyes as I bring water to what's been lying dormant inside you
I want the sweet sounds of your pleasure to open up all doors in which you keep shut
I want to explore you and let me reassure you, I'm not in no rush
I want to love you
So, now I ask again. Can I lay with you?
Can I caress you, before we make love

A Little Girls Cry

Did you ever think of me while I was away?
There wasn't a day that went by that I didn't dream of you
By the minute, everyday , I longed for you
My heart was unsettled steady yearning for you
I waited and waited thinking maybe I was dreaming
I'm your seed there's no way you could just detach yourself from the physical expression of your own soul
You abandoned me and there for love hasn't lived here since
I needed you , that little girl is ready to raise all hell because of you
She cries a river bank full of pain, the cause is you
Suicidal thoughts of death steady constantly on my mind at this point its consuming me
I felt
I felt, as if maybe I just belonged with you
Depression became my shadow
In and out of consciousness
I lived
Tired to balance myself between the two directions I was being pulled in
I needed you to protect me, you were my savior

Damaged Petals

I knew you when you were pure
How can someone so bright turn into one so damaged, so fragile
I guess it's because your mom wasn't there to pick you up when you fell
Maybe it's your dad's absence never making you feel accepted or beautiful
Now, ten years later you fell victim to a man's fist
Still having to go out in this cold world feeling alone
Cold
Not knowing what to call home
I know you're getting tired of always telling yourself one day it will get better
Longing for a peaceful night
Putting a pretty smile on your face throughout these painful nights
Discover your worth through all the fuss and fight
And you'll see yourself in a different light
Free yourself from these chains of destruction
And be the graceful women I've always known you to be

Your Love

Your presence has been demonstrative to what love is
Now this revelation didn't come to me in an instant
It was a buildup, of positive ammunition
Your love awoken something inside me
It just fit
Like a missing puzzle piece just showed up
Your voice calms my soul
It's like somehow, someway, your heart has apart of me in it
Now that I'm aware of it, I just don't want to break away
On my journey, I'm in need of your assistance
(Ego dissipates)
No matter how hard I try simply just taken a leave of absence
With you there's no over reacting you just get me
Even if I had a guard up against you
It becomes useless
Clothed, yet still, in front of you I lie naked
You give me introspection you're truly a blessing
My heart she sings and dance for you
Sometimes , made me cry a tear or maybe two
I can't help but love myself more and more by just the thought of you
You help me get to know myself
I could never run from you
Even with all my fears and scars
It doesn't matter
My heart, open surgery

Healing has taken place while loving you
Me, as a child, I yearned for this
Your eyes
They act as a light
In the center of four black walls I can't help but come towards you
With you I'm seen
As soon as I knew , I started to notice me too
I no longer wanted to hide your love reacted in my body as my rebirth
Something deep inside a beautiful awakening
Of my true self has been birthed
Hopefully, one day you'll open up to me in this way
Proper emotional exchange

Our Love

Our love is timeless
No expiration
The greatest love, known to date
No explanation, no need for any updating
Nostalgic, can never be out dated
Like the feeling you get when Marvin's playing

Broken Hearted Soul

You think you can love a broken-hearted soul?
How can you?
Everywhere I turn , I was met with a wall
Built out of stone
Is that some love hidden?
Peeking out behind the corner
I must have been mistaken
How can you love ?
You're a broken-hearted soul
The condition of your heart, broken down
At a disease, your heart is not functioning at its proper
capacity
Now the question reveals itself why do you wish to love such a
broken-hearted soul?
I lie still, ego set aside, now in comes the truth

Pure Soul

I was told that nowadays pure souls are hard to come by
Well, I had the honor of crossing paths with one
Someone quite special
This soul made me stop, look, and listen to my heart
I heard it say...
What you see standing before your eyes is something
A masterpiece
A blessing
What lies before your eyes is far more than what your eyes can see
What lies before your eyes is greatness
(Change)
A force to be reckoned with
Power
One who effortlessly flows in one direction with a purpose
A soul whose footsteps are divinely guided into what's supposed to be
It's so much more than what your eyes do see
For you to know the true potential of this soul and what may be
You'll have to look deep within YOUR soul, open your heart, and realize your eyes is not at all what your eyes can see
What lies before your eyes is something
Only if the soul knew, would be , could be on top of the world hidden gem
a millionaire working for above minimum wage a boss under another's management what you see, what I see is a pure soul

Operating under the restrictions and limitations of a human vessel
Greatness that has been materialized into the flesh
way more than average above the rest
it's not a flex its just, this one here is simply..
A force to be reckoned with
When it comes to this particular soul words can't express
His expression is worth way more than the words we were taught
I'm talking the words in which we read in the dictionary
Beyond my vocabulary, beyond what my mind can fathom
Its beyond what I feel and sense
Extraordinary, out of this world
Unorthodox, to the flow and system of humankind
What else can I say, its simply greatness
But, to sum it all up
I had the honor, the privilege, the blessing
Of meeting a pure soul
And so it was

If Home Is Where the Heart Is

Is home where the heart is?
A question to self
If home is where the heart is then mine is a broken one
If home is my heart , it's been broken into a million pieces
If I must admit, maybe a million times
My home is a place I want to escape
When I'm near the sight of it, I plan on how I can run away
Pain, it has a place here
Fear it has taken place here
I always wonder how certain situations come into play
I say it's the living conditions in which I stay
It's because of where I lay, it's a reflection of home what else can I say
A broken one I must add with that being said I know home doesn't have to look or feel like it always been
Today
Today I change the conditions in which I live in present day
Can I ask you is home where your heart is?

A Scar on My Heart

Why does my heart hurt so bad?
It feels as if I'm recovering from a deep scar
Like the tissue that now covers the wound is so sensitive to the touch being ripped open
Why does it ache from pain that still feels like it's trying to be uncovered, discovered
Why does my heart ache so bad
I've been purging the pain of my heart out
The cry of a fragmented soul, a cry from a broken spirit
Crying from a broken home
This is my purging season for me to welcome in what's due to me
I've been blocking my blessings
My home hasn't been made whole, so how can I keep intruders out?
I cry tears from lonely nights that send signals to the heavens like an angel that has taken flight
I can no longer fight others for the battle that I hold inside I have to be at my own recuse I'm in my own fire
I have the role as the center piece
Everything that I do gives life to what surrounds me
Its time I birth my natural self and let be

An Impaired Mind

My mind has become impaired

Digging through closets trying to find something I must have misplaced

I need my peace of mind to be put back in its rightful place

I became obsessed with the persona of my flesh

Gave my power away to outside sources

I was feeding my own illusions

Self-inflicted bruises

Steady Flow Of Self-Love

I'm in need of a steady flow of self-love
One that comforts me at night when I'm feeling alone
One that fills me up so that I'm never feeling low

A steady flow of self-love
One that's not measured up by my status quo
One that feels like my one and only true love

I need steady love from the one I struggle staying committed to
the one I've disregarded for another's love

Why haven't I ever been enough?
You're in need, I am in need
of my own steady flow of
Love

Men Suffer in Silence

I'm so confused as to why you chose to suffer in your own silence

You're killing your own spirit

This old thing here

Ain't working so baby why you keep trying

Been gone so long your heart turned blue

(Jazz man's blues)

One more hit

You'll be through

Flow Of Life

Life

Has a rhythm

A natural state of flow

Seasons

Those seasons are attached to cycles

And after a series of cycles comes the full circle moment

After that

Another season begins

Flow with the rhythm of life

Why Does the River Need The Rain?

Does the river need the rain?
Yes, it does
Why you might say?
Everything needs support
Even though you are life someone, something can't give you the blessing of more?
Does the river need the rain?
I'll say yes it does
If your ever able to witness it
You'll understand
Drop by drop
As it hits the rivers floor it's a collective response
Does the river need the rain I'll say yes
It does

Divine Flow

It's something about the water that makes me think
Gives me life
Makes my inner voice sing
I close my eyes, take a deep breath and I start to see
Start to see myself flowing through life as I hear the water be
I am one with this water
For if I was to always be consistent and navigate my way
through life just as the water flows
I would just be
I could just see
See myself through every situation
I could just be the observer
No longer holding myself captive to what I am experiencing
what I see life as, what I think it should be
I'm hearing the water loud, roaring but still, always moving
In one direction, divine flow of protection

Sitting In The Rain

Sitting in the rain
Everything fades
I just need you here
Sitting in the rain
Soul being fed
April showers been bringing me flowers
Sitting in the rain
I am given the gift of power
God is love, I am love, I was created in representation of You

The Sun & The Moon

The sun light
So bright penetrates the mother's fertile land and plants a precious seed so within
The moon light
Reveals the most sacred parts of me A side of me only you can foresee
No other source can give me what you bring
I can't hide anything from mother she's always near
Present, even if she is unable to be seen
The moon
The sun
They are no different they are one never separated never departed
A sacred language the two energies speak so they are the only two in the knowing
The two, a divine representation of balance and inner strength
The two, showing what man and woman should truly bring

I Wonder

I wonder
What if there was no such thing as success
Money held no value
No such thing as losing or winning
No good or bad
If every problem you can think of just crashed and burned
What would hold enough weight in your life that could actually last?
I'm starting to think the world we live in is not the world we live in at all

Cold Feet

Living with abandonment
Before you go , I'll take off , running for the hills
I'm in need just don't know what for
Got real comfortable being on my own
Right now I'm healing but, I'm oblivious to what
I'm unaware
Waking up feeling reinvigorated
I'm being renovated
My concentration, daily basis
I got places to go and see
The feeling be moving through
my spirit calling me
As high as I can ever go
No limits to the unknown

I'm Stuck

Sometimes , I feel stuck
Feels as if I'm watching the same day go by
As if this is all it is to my life
I desire so much more than this here
I'm ready to make my house a home
I'm tired of living in what I've been calling home
I've grown past this
I envision a life where my foundation is built off of peace and everything that surrounds me
is of love and of well being
I'm ready to make my house a home
Detach from all things that go against what I truly want

I am who I say I am

Will they ever let my people go?
I ask in hopes of abrupt change the journey that I have walked allowed me to see and hear the cry of mankind it has allowed me to feel
Their hearts inspired me to be that change this here is beyond my own desires divine purpose flow is what this is here, nah it ain't no phase
I am greatness, its simply ingrained
My presence speaks like a voice that's in harmony
Greatness, like its engraved on a chain
Yea that's just what they been calling me

Count Your Blessings

Count Your blessings
Cut losses
Came this far so you know there's so much more to see, know and grow
In search of new horizons
You're on the rise
Self-love is where its derived
Let your blessings keep you warm at night
Let your losses be the reason why you appreciate your life
Know even though you've lost you haven't lost a thing at all

Forgiveness

Forgiveness
A gift
A form of love
For self
A chance for more
Forgiveness
A door to freedom
The once more
The breath of fresh air after gasping
A precious gift to one's self

My own Fears

What is there to fear
It's all in my own head
conversations with self is what got me here

I'm afraid
of anything that makes me feel it will bring about abrupt change
and that right there is what got me in this
feeling of shame

I can't fight what's for me
I'll turn around and realize
I walked away letting fear control me

Stressing over the past
knowing I've grown from that person I used to be

Whatever I go through
I want to just find my flow and stick with it
and not send anyone who wants to be here
running for the hills

Iniquity

Iniquity; Grossly unfair, Immortal wickedness

I feel like humanity is lacking, starving from the societal indoctrination over the consciousness, collectively

Substantially unequipped to make anything of substance stick

Can't you see the people are dying suffering from something very common, been stripped of self, made to believe it's worth more to trade in moral code

For disease

I Care For You

You just don't know how much I care for you
You left me out in the cold
I was there for you

Nobody else seemed to notice you drowning, in your own troubled waters I came to the rescue
I spoke life to your heart told you your more than a father
You are first, no matter your circumstances through it all, you have to know where YOU stand

You've been a man with a plan that didn't involve giving yourself a chance , a chance at life
A chance to bring about the proper positive uplifting change into your life you seem to always sacrifice this for another's peace
(Robbery)

Through it all, I still love you one day I hope you give yourself the chance, the space, the opportunity to grow
Grow into the man that's waiting for you on the other side
I feel my heart hurting in your absence
(You're not around)

I'm in Love

I am so in love with you
The way you walk, talk, speak, and do
Magnetic
It just seems to draw me in, closer to you
Even with all that you've been through, your strength is warrior status.
This physical world can't break you
Heaven sent; made with careful intent
Knew exactly what they were doing when they made you
You fail to realize what you made it through
Bullet wounds left from bullets shot through you yet, your still hustling that didn't even phase you
You never let circumstances change you
Day in day out stayed down
That's one of the reasons I praise you a heart made of pure gold
Yet, worth so much more I'm truly amazed by you

My Motivation

Baby you keep me going
You keep me in love
You lift me up when I've been beating myself down
If I was to trip you would catch me right before I hit the ground
You are my air when I forget to breathe
My rain when I feel I'm going into my dry season
You are my wake call, welcoming my due season

Save Me

Won't you save me
Going under
Rushing escaping demons been in my head
I'm over thinking
Times I felt I couldn't take it
Felt myself slipping away
Self-destruction
My bright light that was you
Swept me up and saved me from the drowning
I was giving up
You saved me
I'm asking
Wondering
Hoping
This time, will you save me again

Subconscious Dump

I'm no longer living in fear
Its time I let go of the anchor that's been pulling me down
I feel like I'm moving different
My mind is saying one thing and yet my mouth follows and says another
I'm moving out of my subconscious beliefs
I know there's parts of me that are unseen hidden in my shadows but show up in my everyday routine
I'm aware that I'm in need of a dump
No longer going to be operating from dead parts of my being.
From this dump , new life will start to bud